THE DOLPHIN HOUSE

O'Brien

ISBN: 978-1-913642-37-2

Book designed by Aaron Kent

Edited by Aaron Kent

Broken Sleep Books (2021), Talgarreg, Wales

In 1965, a bottlenose dolphin christened Peter was the subject of a scientific experiment. For six weeks, he lived in a flooded apartment in the Virgin Islands with a woman named Margaret Howe, who was tasked with teaching him human language.

All hands on deck.
    The sea thrashing below
a crew of Cretan sailors,
        bound for gold.

    In a flotation tank,
        the god Apollo
    crests the black brine.

        Thought is a surging shoal:
          whistles and clicks.

    Outside of Biddeford, Maine,
a huge brain throbs
        to death on a coastal road.

    Men come with saws.

        Someone like Aristotle
      walking the shore
         gazed at the gleaming blue.

It saw him too.   *Hello*, it said. *Hello.*

You & me & the incredibly distant island universes

The man behind the glass removes his gloves.
The man without his gloves, glittered in salt,
flips up his goggle glasses, and he looks
like a woodsman training as a legal clerk,
tucked tightly in his suit — savage and tall.
His pockets brim with pens. His notes are damp.
He cracks the door.

                 You want to speak to me?

When John drinks coffee, and he does drink coffee,
it's squid-ink black and his jitter's justified.
That's how we do it in St. Paul, he says,
but tell me about you.

                           I tried.
I tried to hold my threadbare quilt of life —
some college, and a few hostessing shifts —
up to him, and he burnt through and charged on.
He told me that he was a journalist.
No, that's not right, he said. A generalist,
which seemed concerned with keeping people sane,
although of course (he said) so few of us are.

Stubs in the ashtray. Grey mulch in the cup.

If you could see into my soul, John said,
assuming that you think the soul exists,
what would you see?
                       I didn't know.

He told me, and it was a litany:
the miles from Como to Cathedral Hill;
the baseball stats for 1934;
the fields of science and psychology,

13

all overlapping like a magic eye;
the words of Christ, of Huxley and Karl Marx,
and how it felt to drive a well-built car,
guide in your hand a finely-made machine;
genetics as a branch of moral law,
and fucking as epistemology —

he used that word. Epistemology.
Asked me to wait for him to finish work.

I hold the joint like a laser
scanning the surface of the moon.
John bathes in thought, while I just

slowly

pulse

and what he says is *Margaret, your mind —*
with all its files and drawers, all its dark rot —
has barely opened up onto itself.
You're still so young. I like it that you're young,
but how — and tell me this — how can we hope
to know, to truly know, the dolphin's mind
when all we understand about ourselves
is echoes, ego — a rat stuck in a tube
never suspecting life whirls on outside —
when we so feebly sound our own still depths,
how can we reach another consciousness?

The mirror in the car is all his eyes.

I didn't know. I said I didn't know.

Grand mal

That dolphin diddled itself to death, John said,
eyes glazed — Marineland, 1957.
They'd drilled a steel sleeve into its head
and let it push the lever with its beak
to trigger — whistles, barks, Bronx cheers; a jammed switch.
Then blasts of airborne phonemes. Bounced from heaven,
its killing lack had stunned him into speech,
like pleasure was the origin of language.

That's how it was when John was called to science.
Alone on the farm with his father's exercise belt,
aged ten, he buckled into the appliance.
Waves of the purest bliss he'd ever felt:
Godlike vibrations. Shamed, he swore: *The truth
is wider than any damned confession booth.*

Let us improve ourselves

John says the sperm whale has religious ambitions.
He's scared that China's developing the bomb.

A rat fell into the tank and nobody drowned him:
the only response from those jaws,
a curious prod of sound.

Something is forming inside me the shape of love,
or the Golden Rule: an untranslatable ethic
beyond our current capacity for kindness.

If we want to speak to Alpha Eridani,
and I think we do, then something here has to shift.

Independent vocal work

Babies form words before knowing their meanings:
this fact does not diminish their eagerness.
On such assumptions, we already agree.

Dolphins, like humans, can plan ahead,
their big minds sloshing towards the future.
They will not let us see this without trust.

I have an idea and I want to share that idea.
Let's plaster the whole damn place.
Sure, go ahead and joke about immersion:

I'm used to being interrupted now.
Roll down that garage door and drive away; those brains
lie wasting in the water all night long.

I am not a zoologist or a psychoanalyst.
Perhaps my comments are basic, but they are sound.
I am prepared to give this 1000 hours;

give this my life. (I practice in front of the mirror.)
You've seen the spectrograms — we're well beyond
operant conditioning. The bobo clown

falls down; springs up. Everyone's getting ulcers.
My eyes are as open as they possibly can be,
and I have never wanted anything more.

Wet courage

An early morning storm, and John downstairs
standing like some Midwestern Prospero
before the boiling, crashing water. Stars
the only light on glinting skin. Below,
Tursiops turned in unison — observed
but unaffected. John himself the same:
thoughts in the distance with the deep sea surge —
alone, he thought, until I said his name.

He asked me if I'd seen it: his stark fear
for their small pod, with every wave a shark —
and then its vanishing, like going clear,
as he perceived their calm, their comfort. *Yes.*
Which is why I think we should embark
on something new here...   Hungry for his blessing.

A special pool in a special room in a special building

A house located at the water line.	[X]
A depth of at least eighteen inches.	[X]
A gate not operable by sharks, sawfish or octopuses.	[X]
Thoroseal and trade wind waves.	[X] [X]
Plaques for the 'classroom': color, number, shape.	[X]

A Wollensak and Crown lavalier microphone, shipped in from Minnesota M&M, with tapes. [X]

Chain hoist with shackle; I-beam monorail; foam pallet, doubling as mattress; swing, and ropes. [X]

Leotards and tights.	[X]
Youngness of spirit; an ability to improvise.	[X]
The vacuum from Miami.	[X] *(small mouth.)*
Bras without hooks; these tend to wilt.	*(A problem.)*
Dry clothes, sheets, towels, blankets.	*(As far as possible.)*
Deep water; shallow; dry.	[X] [X] *(desirable.)*
A six-foot pool to be a dolphin in.	[X]
Human zone (for relaxation as a human.)	[X]
A mutually-adapting area.	[X]
A swivel chair. A TV set covered in polyethylene.	[X] [X]
Wall carpet.	[X]
Pen, paper, desk. High shelves for storage.	[X]
Four-poster-style shower curtains.	[X]

115-volt lights, with the switch and cables in a separate room. [X] [X]

Two-burner gas stove. Tinned spaghetti.	[X]
Saltwater toothpaste.	[X]
Fifteen to twenty pounds of butterfish per day.	[X]
With more for human operator.	[X]

Everyone loves to talk to a baby

A ball, a Ba Bee block, a bobo clown.
A burst of sound.
Tell me your name —
all things should have a name.

A learn, a lapse.
Bring ball, turn tail
for tummy rubs.
A broom to ward him off during my meal.

Colour is tough, understandably.
We spend the morning greeting,
you & me — *hello, hello*!
The schedule says: *Relax,* and so we do.

B-b-b-b-b-b-b-b-b-brush!
Demands and diamonds.
Soon I'll find a way
of siphoning the milky water clean.

Why let the water get in the way?

And Peter rested on the seventh day.
I bundled him into the elevator;
he rode it like a businessman. *Go, play,*
boy, play. Brief bliss. Then, twelve hours later,
he'd rise again, more muted in his thrashing,
and I'd put down my damp-edged diary,
sink back into his world. Almost blushing,
I'd wade to welcome back this ball of need.
Down in the sea pool, Pamela and Sissy
would click behind my back, or else they'd mock
that clumsy merboy, rough-skinned, and his fussing
whine of separation from me in the dark.
But how was I to grasp the things they said?
Or they, that I was up here on this bed?

Humanoiding

John Lovett, the photographer, came by.
A treat for me, and so, perhaps,
for primadonna Peter,
after all these weeks:
our study in dyadic isolation.

Constant contact; lagging pumps;
a bone-deep numbness in my knees;
high fever, and a lack of polythene.
I envy the microphones in plastic bags
hanging like meat from the ceiling.

Sometimes I think I'll never be that dry again.

Last Friday I got in the car, and drove and drove
until the radio could scour my brain
clear of its delphinese.
The old hotel on the savage bluff: so tedious.
A person isn't meant to live like this.

Which, to his credit, Lovett didn't say —
he passed over the algae and the Thoroseal
in tender, working silence, broken up with clicks.
Nice home you're making here — showed in my smile, I think,
before Peter came charging through the Dutch door.

It's pleasant to be understood for once.

Fourth of July

Of course he wouldn't wear a hat.
Of course the soggy tickertape.
Of course this can of frosting in the dark,

water-light softening its jagged edges,
and for just a tick I seriously thought:
what if I slit his throat?

The body bundled in the elevator.
Blood spreading like a firework,
like neurons forming, point by point,

until it reached the grouting.
Richard and Aubrey, my dry boys,
kept laughing when they slapped it on the walls,

asking which one of us had chosen
the shade of paint: me,
or the herring hog?

Nothing from John, or even from
that other, kinder John —
my diligent recorder.

I guess he won't be checking up on me.
I turned the set up. Peter yawped
'My Country, Tis Of Thee.'

My saturated bed; a second, mermaid puberty.
His jealous shrieks when my mother phoned.
You can always come home.

I gave my lesson. I wrung out the flag.
Five weeks, and he can't count to three.
Some holiday.

I spent it scrubbing algae from the walls,
a bad joke in a spangled leotard
as Peter threw himself

against the barriers of language,
battering my legs with a persistence
that was almost human.

A very precious sort of thing

audible "pop."
extrusion from
the genital groove.
penis rubbing,
fully erect, on leg.
perineal stimulation
offered, to subjective
pre-ejaculatory state.
peduncle fluke
held oddly still.
left eye closed.
eye opened.
peduncle fluke
moved gently down.
inevitability.
positive stimuli
overcome inhibitors,
exciting neurons
in the spinal cord,
relaying signals
to the brain,
prompting secretion;
motor efferent discharge.
womp. womp.
contraction of
the epididymis
and vesicles;
involuntary pumping
of the bulbocavernosus.
dense seminal fluid
ejected from the tip.
pulsive emission.
muscle stretched up.
(all this repeated twice.)

Theoretical biology

If I could have my fingers fuse, I would.
If I could pin my ears flat, I would,
and press my nostrils up towards my hairline; sprout
a dorsal fin the colour of a prom dress.

If I could be like you, I'd surely try —
all smoothness, fat and resonant with echoes.
But Peter, is there something I've done wrong?
When did you drift so far away from me?

You have warm blood like mine: this much I know,
and if you want to breathe, you can't stay down there.
I've dipped more than a flipper in your world —
wishing you'd only surface, that you'd share.

Our best minds

Then Bateson takes me aside,
on the understanding that I —
a woman in my mid-20s,
no letters after my name —
can't simply take aside
the founding funder of the CRI,
and he says *John's in the long grass.*
John's stepped out too deep.

He slides a tape across to me,
beginning at 5.56pm, marked "Peter LSD":
hard evidence that John had done
the one thing which he promised not to do.
I listen later to the stillness,
or as John would have it,
sound that has *no meaning in the verbal sphere.*

What Bateson says has meaning.
This has gone too far —
beyond barbiturates,
beyond productive therapeutic work,
beyond the realm of science.
He's using words like *prudent* and *endangerment*,
stroking my bare arm in
a way I don't receive as reassuring.

I picture Pam and Sissy,
eyes gone glassy, floating soporifically
as buoyant taxidermy,
and I have to concede
this is the opposite of communication.
All I can find to say is, *Not my boy.*

Everything will, apparently, be taken care of.
There is no reason to fret, as if I ever have.
He reiterates that they see me as the ideal mother;

that neither of them would ever have had the patience.
I am being very patient now.

At least he doesn't pretend
there will still be a place for me;
some consolation for
the slight smirk on those lips which I would swear
have never tasted butterfish.
I hold back brine.
Margaret, he says,
it's time to pull the plug.

Survival computations

Take down the hanging carpets — squeeze them dry,
and roll them tight. Then dump out all the fish.
Winch down the desk. No desk should be that high.
There, in the normal place — install a wall switch.

Throw out the sling, the leotard; the hoist
might be of use on some construction site.
(Lovett comes by to help, and Peter's voice
squalls softer in my ears. He finds the good light.)

Brick up the dolphin door, then run the hose.
Run cables in. Stop if you hear a buzz.
I like it here — still. Lovett nods. Exposed,
the bed — we both see — looks ridiculous.

I would recommend that this planet be shunned

John gets a letter from the former bank
in Florida, where someone who was once
almost my boyfriend lay deposited.
I can't imagine how they'd have arranged the space:
the meeting place, the mutually-adapting area.
Tanks by the tellers' counter? High as that, or higher?
Does he have the length and breadth required to play?
A ball? A block? Is my name on his lips?

John, on the phone (and not the John who helped
my last days packing up the lab,
the John behind the shower curtain now)
folds up the letter, fiddles with a paperweight,
and tells me Peter has drowned himself
by voluntarily ceasing to breathe,
sinking to the fetid bottom,
in what a human coroner might,
under sufficient pressure,
have written off as death by misadventure —
and so write off how water might arrange
its motion like a shroud, holding his body under
helplessly; its innocence enfolding him,
until he sank beneath the shifting surface which
he never learnt it was his place to break.

> *Dolphins in close contact with men are infected by direct handling.*
> *A sick dolphin does not eat.*
> *An ill dolphin should not be left in solitude.*

We can't know what he thought, John says,
which at the time doesn't strike me as insanity.
(My John sits next to me and numbly soothes.)
When my eyes lift the scientist is talking
about the magpies settling in his yard
on Selby Avenue; how as a kid

40

he managed to outsmart the counting rhyme.
They weren't all in the same place — well, so what?
That didn't mean I was stuck with sorrow.

That one dark omen was a hurdle to clear,
not a sign to stop adding, trying.
The bank will dispose of the remains, he says,
the word clearly chosen calmly. A regrettable loss,
but far away. They have municipal facilities.
You do what you want, Margaret, he says, fixing
what sounds like a mid-afternoon piña colada.
I prefer to operate a cumulative magpie policy.

Man said things not

After the splash in *Hustler*, that was that.
Forget it. We were more than sex. This place,
which liquid hasn't lapped in forty years,
was more: we raised three daughters here.
But sometimes, still, sat in my patterned TV chair,
no polythene in sight, I catch reflections.

Altered States? I didn't get a line in *Altered States.*
That was all John in tanks, half-nude,
a raging monk's magnetic selfishness.
He throbs into his caveman form like lumpy bread,
then flirts with phasing into sentient light.
Love pulls him back, at last.

Mike Nichols thought that love explained it, too.
He married us; gave Peter his own partner;
let us learn and live, despite the fact
we taught a living creature its first lie.
The ball is bad — redeemed beneath Ben Franklin's bust.
More palm-frond beach huts, though, and more verandas.

Worst of them all is this, uploaded to
your stupid website: *Maui, Earth.*
Your disco suit, your coonskin cap — a broken brain,
happy by then to simply find an audience.
A wunderkind who soured into a charlatan,
swimmer who never heard the calls from shore.

Extraction, not love, is the shape I recognise.
You mining anything in the universe —
space, Polynesia, karma, chemistry —
if it could keep you talking. He can't speak.
I don't know where his body is.
You only know the ones you think you've hurt.

1965

That was a time of gills:
you only had to throw a rock
to find a man slitting his neck
and bounding into the deep,
dreaming that he could float
attached to nothing —

nothing but mystic science.
We were on top of the world
and we were below,
flinging our messages out like paint
across the Atlantic,
casting a disc through space

like a compact mirror. No —
like a boomerang.
All those days we spent
seeking beyond ourselves,
confident any signal we could receive
would use a language we could speak

or a mouth that could be trained.
Homo aquaticus was a party costume;
a wetsuit, really,
where the implants came
out of your cheek like dentures.
Sure, contact would change us —

but not immeasurably. You could still keep
your bank account, your name,
and if they responded at all
to the call they'd come
to see it our way —
to join us, John.

No one was meant to stay.

CCCCCXXXXXCCXXXX XXX

so say
I start to talk the way
you want me to

and say I speak
about those over-water weeks
what would it mean to you

this vocal suit
this crawl
towards the vertical

now the Cetacean Chair
will take the floor
and tell you   what

you want to hear
that you were right
you saw me through the aquatint

but if my world
was too wide and too wild
to shunt

into the traps of consonants
and I began
to make you understand

what would you see
the sea
meeting the logic of the land

swallows and burns
and goes away
and the land learns

nothing it holds
nothing that fits
into the vessels carved for it

this minstrelsy
this passing soon
is meaningless beneath the moon

which sways my home
which holds me down
which is itself reflected light

on the wrong side
of a long night
so say

I rose   sublunary
and sleeved with rays
you cannot see

and say my secrets
rose up too
in words that meant nothing to you

and say my story
whistled burst
through your unhearing universe

incomprehensible and free
untameable as smoke
and say I spoke

Acknowledgements

This sequence of poems, some of which have appeared in previous forms in *The White Review, Wild Court, bath magg* and *The Lyrical Aye,* is a blend of fact and fiction. I make no special claims to knowledge about the inner lives of Margaret Howe, John Lilly, or of course Peter the dolphin, beyond what I have acquired from previous accounts of their time together (including previous fictions).

These include, but are not limited to, *The Mind of the Dolphin*, by Lilly himself and containing some of Howe's own notes on the experiment; the documentary *The Girl Who Talked to Dolphins,* by Christopher Riley; Breach Theatre's production of *Tank; Voices in the Ocean,* by Susan Casey; *The Sounding of the Whale,* by D. Graham Burnett; William Poundstone's biography, *Carl Sagan: A Life in the Cosmos;* Ken Russell's film *Altered States; The Day of the Dolphin,* directed by Mike Nichols with screenplay by Buck Henry; and my first vocal lesson, 'Hello,' an episode of the podcast *Radiolab* produced by Lynn Levy.

Many of the poem titles are taken verbatim from Lilly's book, and lines in a number of the poems also draw directly on his unusually extravagant language, as well as Howe's descriptions of her experience. Lines appear from *Altered States* and *The Day of the Dolphin*: particularly in 'Man Said Things Not,' which also owes a linguistic debt to conversations with my partner Sydnee Wagner. However, much here is also invented, in a conscious attempt to inhabit imaginatively, some fifty-five years later, the strange mental and social landscapes in which the CRI experiments took place. All responsibility for divergence from the truth on those grounds lies entirely with me.

LAY OUT YOUR UNREST

Lightning Source UK Ltd.
Milton Keynes UK
UKHW020018070121
376414UK00005B/66